JASON CASTILLE

TATE PUBLISHING
AND **ENTERPRISES**, LLC

Published by Tate Publishing & Enterprises, LLC
127 E. Trade Center Terrace | Mustang, Oklahoma 73064 USA
1.888.361.9473 | www.tatepublishing.com

Tate Publishing is committed to excellence in the publishing industry. The company reflects the philosophy established by the founders, based on Psalm 68:11,
"The Lord gave the word and great was the company of those who published it."

Book design copyright © 2013 by Tate Publishing, LLC. All rights reserved.
Cover design by Jim Villaflores
Interior design by Jomel Pepito

Published in the United States of America

ISBN: 978-1-62994-027-4
1. Family & Relationships / Marriage
2. Self-Help / General
13.11.25

Dedication

To my lovely wife Rebecca, she has supported me through thick and thin, for richer or for poorer, in sickness and in health. She has faithfully endured my long absences while I was away at war in Iraq, and then while I was sick and wounded in distant hospitals. She is definitely my better half and I could not have survived without her.

I would also like to mention my kids, who have been very patient and have endured great adversity while I was serving in the army during Operation Iraqi Freedom. When I got home, I spent years in and out of distant hospitals, and I was away for a very long time. I never heard them complain. They supported me and served their country honorably, and I thank each and every one of them.

Contents

Introduction

You can search high and low, to the east and to the west, to the north and to the south, but no matter how hard you search, no doubt, you'll be hard pressed to find a woman like my wife. When God made her, he "broke the mold," just like the old saying goes.

In the reality of life, things are not like you see in the movies, or read about in fairy tales. In marriages, there are good times and bad times; there are high times and low times. There will be times when you fight and times when it's right. All of this is normal in marriage. The key objective is to know how to respond.

I wrote this book to offer hope to men who think that their marriage is hopeless; for men who think that things are too far gone to fix them. And they have drifted so far apart that they think there is no hope of reconnecting. Rest assured my friend, there is always hope, especially if you approach marriage from a biblical perspective. The Bible tells us how to treat our wives. It also instructs our wives how to treat us. When we follow these principles, our marriages can flourish.

I know that if my wife and I can stay together after what we've been through, then so can you. Just take a look at this scripture, "And we know that in all things God works for the good of those who love him, who have been called according to his purpose" (Romans 8:28, NIV). Say that out loud five times. Good job, now remember that this applies to your marriage too.

I believe your marriage will never be the same after you read this book. You will be praying together, staying together, laughing together, and praising the Lord all the way to the bank of good times together.

I will give you helpful hints to get things going in the bedroom. In fact, if you spend a little less time watching that box with all the channels on it, and spend more time paying attention to the lady that you married, you will find that she has some interesting buttons as well, and if you will quit complaining that she cut you off, and cut that television off, you might find that the off button to the television set is the "on" button to your wife. Try it, it works. I have a lot of other helpful hints too, so start reading this book. You will lose some calories, relieve some stress, and have a great time in the process.

This book will truly help you to have *your best wife now.*

Your Money or Your Wife

If you were out for a leisurely walk about town with your wife and a rather tall, smelly creature of a man pointed a gun at you and demanded, "Your money or your wife" which would you gives him? If you answered money, then you are on the right track already, good job. Your wife should always come first, after God of course, but as far as humans go, it should be your wife.

On the other hand, if it took all of five seconds to fork over your better half, that's right, and she smells better too, then read on buddy this book's for you. You see, your priorities are backwards, and that's okay because the fact that you purchased this book tells me that there is a change blowing in the wind.

In addition, I think it's only right to say that your wife should come even before your children. Why? I am glad you asked. You see, one day, all of your children will grow up, and move out, and that will leave you all alone with guess who? Yep, you're catching on, you're pretty smart. What will happen if you spend all of your children's lives paying strict attention to their every desire, and always giving them your best, while your wife gets put on the back burner? The answer is that in the end, you will be living all alone, with a complete stranger. While loving our kids is important, we have to maintain a balance which includes nurturing your wife.

There is an old saying that states, "You get out of life, what you put into it." It is the same with marriage; you get out of a "wife" what you put in to her so to speak.

Your wife is a gift from God. When you take her home and unwrap her, don't forget how special she is. She deserves your respect and needs your respect. If you show her respect, she will give it in return.

As husbands, we need to remember that we have been assigned by God as the ones to set the examples of how things should go in the household. The husband is the spiritual leader. If the husband doesn't assume this role, then the wife usually has to. This really messes things up, especially when children are involved. When they see Mom playing both roles, they get confused.

God wired us a certain way for a reason and when we act outside of these "lines," chaos is sure to follow. If Dad doesn't go to church, but Mom makes the kids go with her, when they get old enough to decide for themselves, they will tend to follow Dad's example. Fortunately by then, they will have heard enough of God's word to return to him when they mature as adults, but a lot of damage can occur in the meantime. "Train a child in the way he should go, and when he is old he will not turn from it" (Proverbs 22:6, NIV).

For example, they will tend to experiment in the world to see what it has to offer in the form of alcohol, sex, pornography, drugs, etc. I've been there; I know what I am talking about, trust me.

It is written in the Bible, "For the husband is the head of the wife as Christ is the head of the church, his body, of which he is the Savior" (Ephesians 5:23, NIV). This is a huge responsibility, and one that should not be taken lightly. I should further state that this is not a God-given clearance for abusive behavior either. Mutual respect by both parties is important.

The Bible also says,

> Husbands, love your wives, just as Christ loved the church and gave himself up for her to make her holy, cleansing her by the washing with water through the Word, and to present her to himself as a radiant church, without stain or wrinkle or any other blemish, but holy and blameless. In this same way, husbands ought to love their wives as their own bodies. He who loves his wife loves himself
>
> (Ephesians 5:25-28 NIV).

I find these verses to be very moving. It really gives us a clear picture of how we should treat our wives. I feel like it is not a weakness to treat your wife like a queen. It is not a weakness to open the door for her, or to help her with her chair at the table. Besides, it takes more of a man to treat a woman right, than it does to treat her wrongly.

It is time for the divorce rate to lower in this world, and the only way it is going to happen is for men to take the lead role in the family unit. It takes us making the first move. We must be the ones taking the initiative. We were placed in this position by God. It is time we took the matter into our own hands. If we do this, we can change the world, one family at a time.

I realize that it is not in our "manly" nature to be sensitive and soft. This is something that we have to acquire with a little effort on our part. As men, we tend to come home from work and kick the wife and kiss the dog, and then retire into our caves so we can stare blankly at the television and tune out everything our wives say to us the entire evening, with the exception of "supper is ready." I know this because I am guilty of this very thing. I have done it the wrong way for years and it only leads to misery. So I am preaching to myself too.

For those of you who are not taking your wives to church and are not taking the spiritual lead in your home, the fact that you're reading this book makes my heart jump for joy, and I am proud that you care enough about your wife to want to make your marriage better.

Points to Ponder

- ✓ If a big smelly man approaches you on the street and demands your money or your wife, give him your money.
- ✓ Your wife comes before your children.
- ✓ Your children will move out one day, so it is important to maintain a wonderful relationship with your wife so she won't be a stranger when they do.
- ✓ Your wife is a gift from God.
- ✓ God and your relationship with Jesus come before your wife so that you can be the spiritual leader of the home that God made you to be.
- ✓ You get out of life what you put in to it and you get out of marriage what you put in to it.
- ✓ Don't let your wife forget how special she is.
- ✓ "Husbands, love your wives just as Christ loved the church. He who loves his wife loves himself" (Ephesians 5:25, NIV).
- ✓ It is not a weakness to treat your wife like a queen.
- ✓ It takes more of a man to treat a woman right than to treat a woman wrong.
- ✓ It is time for the divorce rate to lower and the only way it is going to happen is for men to start putting their wives second only to God.
- ✓ We have to make the first move.

- ✓ We must take the initiative.
- ✓ God put us in this position.
- ✓ It is time we take the wheel, and start changing the world one family at a time.

Dirty Laundry

How many of you guys out there have attempted to surprise your wife by doing her laundry? Am I the only one? I feel so embarrassed. I mention this story to point out that there are some things you can do for your Queen that you think are helpful, that turn out the opposite.

For instance, when I first married my wife, I decided to wash some clothes. I walked around and picked up my underwear off of the floor, (I figured that alone would earn me some points) then I found a couple of pair of dirty jeans here and there, and a towel or two. I then thought, *Hey, I'll surprise my wife and throw in a couple of her sweaters, and maybe a blouse or two.*

So here I go in my state of ignorant bliss, whistling while I work, picturing how my queen is going to be proud of her handsome man when she gets home, and thinking of the special favors I am going to receive that night. I had a spring in my step and a song in my heart. I opened the lid on that mysterious machine with all the fancy knobs, and I crammed all of the above-mentioned items forcefully into it, thinking that the more force I used, the cleaner the clothes would get. I thought it looked pretty neat too because of the vast array of colors. So I thought what this colorful load must need is superhot water to get the items super clean.

In addition to the superhot water, I figured if just a little bit of highly concentrated detergent worked as good as the container said, then a mega dose of the super concentrated detergent would work five times better, so I went with the super-mega manly dose. I slapped the door shut, and I let this wonderful machine go to work.

The hot water roared like the river wild. The steam was so thick; you could cut it with a knife. The aroma of detergent filled the air. The motor roared into life and the agitator began to agitate, then it drained, then more water, then more agitation, then it drained again, then came the spin cycle. What an invention the washing machine is. I remember being in Iraq, and washing my clothes in a bucket; this is when we had water to spare. Otherwise, it was wear your clothes until they could stand up by themselves. It kind of made a fellow walk like a robot and smell like road kill. Not a pretty sight or smell I can tell you that much.

Anyway, when the clothes were finished washing, and I convinced myself to get out of my easy chair, and quit channel surfing like a zombie, I started for the washer. When I am channel surfing, I look like a fifties style surfer on steroids. Upon arrival at the washing machine, I managed to extricate the clothes without the aid of the Jaws of Life. The clothes were shaken but stable, and I figured I needed to apply some more heat before they went into shock. I found the nearest dryer, and I quickly inserted the items into it and cranked the dial over to sixty minutes on high heat. I thought I was helping okay? I went back to my remote, and after watching some cowboys get in a bar fight and a group of castaways try to get off of an island, the buzzer was going off.

So here I go to retrieve the clothes. I grabbed a pair of my jeans and folded them, no problem. Then I grabbed a pair of my underwear and chunked them in the basket, no problem. Next I picked up one of my wife's blouses, and there was a big problem. Didn't this blouse used to be white? I was pretty sure that it went in to the washer white, and when the clothes got transferred they were damp, and I did not notice a change but now there is a serious anomaly here in the control tower. I was thinking that it used to be bigger too.

Now I don't know if my queen has ESPN, or if it was just a case of bad timing, but she walked in the house right during the folding operation. In a nervous act of desperation I said, "Hello honey, guess what I'm doing"? She said something along the lines of, "I don't know dear, I'm afraid to ask."

Then it happened. She spotted a blouse, then a sweater. Then she scanned the clothes and noted the jeans and towels and all of the rest of the prohibited items that had been washed with her precious blouse and sweaters.

Have you ever seen the lid blow off of a pressure cooker? My queen proceeded to lecture me and line me out like a drill instructor does a private. She chewed me up one side and then down the other. She made it quite clear then and there the dos and don'ts of washing clothes. But the biggest don't of all was, "Don't ever wash my clothes again!" I said "yes Madam" and "you're welcome." Boy howdy did I ever learn a huge lesson on that fateful day.

So, if you are reading this and you are a newlywed, remember this story if your wife goes shopping on a Saturday and you're home alone feeling industrious. Don't wash her clothes! You can mow the lawn, take out the trash, wash the driveway, water the yard, feed the dog, fix the fence, and phone a friend. Just don't get near her clothes. She will also advise you to never wash in hot water, even though as a man, it only makes sense that the hotter the water the cleaner the clothes. They may get cleaner, but the hot water ruins the shape or something. Cold water is the key. Don't use too much detergent. Don't use dish soap in the washing machine, or the dishwasher either, you will have foam all over the wash-room and/or kitchen.

Just try to remember, that there are some things that are better left undone. So there you have it. Our queens can be very complicated. They can think about twenty different things at one time. They can talk on the phone, talk to their kids in the house, wash dishes, and chew gum, while reading *Good Housekeeping* at the same time. We men can normally only think about, and do one thing at a time, and if we are on a certain task, we will not go on to anything else until we finish that task. Anything that interrupts this process can totally drive us crazy. Finding ways to get these two different beings to function together and get along is not always easy, but it is possible. Keep on reading. You are doing great. You will be a pro by the time you finish this book. I am confident that you will. It takes a real man to take the initiative that you are taking to make sure that your marriage stays solid.

Points to Ponder

- ✓ There are some things that you can do for your queen that you think is helpful.
- ✓ Do not wash your queen's laundry without her express written or oral consent.
- ✓ If you do get her consent, pay close attention to the instructions. There are some things that are not to be washed in hot water and there are some items that are not to be dried.
- ✓ Do not mix colors please.
- ✓ Mow the lawn.
- ✓ Plant a garden.
- ✓ Take out the trash.
- ✓ Wash the car.

- ✓ Keep it safe.
- ✓ It is great to be helpful as long as you know what you are doing.

Try the following:

List some things below that you can do for your wife that will make her happy, that you can't mess up.

_____

_____

_____

_____

_____

_____

_____

_____

Keep in mind that your wife is unique. What may upset one wife may not upset another, and then there are things that upset all wives.

You know your wife better than anyone. If you are newlyweds, just watch and learn what type of a wife you have, and then adjust accordingly.

Based on what you know up to this point about her, pick some things that you can do around your house that you can't mess up and list them below.

_____

_____

_____

_____

_____

_____

_____

_____

Try them and pick out the ones that are successful and the ones that are not. Then give each item a rating based upon how your spouse reacts. Then you can use these results as a guide to regulate how to make your wife happy.

Example:

1. Action: Made the bed.

   Response: Wife was overjoyed, and gave me a big kiss, and promised me a special favor tonight.

2. Action: Mowed the yard.

Response: Wife said I noticed you mowed the yard, it's about time.

So write down a list of things you can think of to do below, and then get a separate sheet of paper or an index card or your favorite electronic device to keep a record of what responses you get.

_____

_____

_____

_____

_____

_____

_____

_____

Over time, you will begin to know how to regulate the happiness in your household. The object is to keep the wife happy. We have all heard and know that if the wife isn't happy then nobody's happy. I'm just trying to help you, brother.

Washing Dishes

Now my dear friend, this issue is a bit complicated, but if done correctly, it can pay off big time in rewards. The thing to keep in mind is that there are two ways to wash dishes. You can use the dishwasher, which for a man can spell trouble, or you can wash them by hand. Why am I writing about washing dishes? You will see, just keep reading.

Let me address the dishwasher, I know it sounds simple right? You just open her up, throw the dishes in, add the detergent, close the door, and turn the knob to wash. Wow, now that was quick and simple, my wife is going to be so proud. Not so fast there buddy, you can wind up in a bind real easy when you to try to take advantage of the latest in kitchen technology. Especially when you don't have a clue what you are doing. If you think your sweetheart is going to find this sexy, then think again Romeo, she won't.

The good thing is that if you mess up washing dishes, it is not nearly as bad as messing up washing the queen's clothes. With the dishes, you can do them over and over again until you get them right. You may be asking yourself what in the heck is wrong with washing the dishes in the way that was just described? The answer is, absolutely nothing, if you're a single male. However, women have to make sure the dishwasher is operated in just a certain way, or it is *w-r-o-n-g!*

First of all, you can't just take a dirty dish and chunk it in the dishwasher. You must first scrape all of the food off and then wash it in the sink. I know it defeats the whole purpose of having a dishwasher; that's what I said too. Anyway, now you can place the dish on the wash rack.

Now, can you place the dishes just anywhere you want to? No way, this will upset the queen quicker than you can say deer hunting. She will come behind you and make a scene over your loading job, and give you a class right there in the kitchen.

You must put all the matching plates neatly together in a row. You must have the saucers together, the bowls together, the glasses, the cups, and the different types of silverware all placed neatly according to its kind (like Noah's Ark). If anything is wrong, the queen will find it.

So, if you are going to have to wash the dishes in the sink anyway, why even use the dishwasher I say.

Now let's get to the fun part. My wife let me in on some top secret information. Are you ready for this? Women find it sexy to watch their husband standing at the sink washing dishes. So therefore, if I am going to wash dishes, I am going to do it the old fashion way.

That's it, just put the remote down and step away from the recliner, go scrub some dishes, surprise your honey, and take a load off of her tonight. I bet you, she will return the favor in a way that you would appreciate. It would not hurt to call the flower shop and order some roses either. We need to keep the romance going. It does not matter how long you have been married, if you treat each day like it is the first day, then the sparks will keep flying. If you are just getting started and the sparks are hot and heavy, then keep it that way. Mix things up so you don't get in a particular rut. Always look for new and interesting ways to surprise your loved one, and your marriage won't get dull.

Furthermore, it would not hurt to take a hint from Solomon and throw in a verse such as, "How beautiful you are my darling! Oh, how beautiful! Your eyes are doves" (Song of Songs 1:15). Try it! Wash some dishes, and quote some Solomon, and see what happens.

Points to Ponder

- ✓ There are two ways to wash dishes, either by hand or the dishwasher.
- ✓ The dishwasher can spell trouble for a man.
- ✓ Washing by hand can be good for a man.
- ✓ You can wind up in a bind when you try to use the latest in kitchen technology.

- ✓ Messing up on washing dishes is not nearly as bad as messing up by washing the queen's clothes.
- ✓ You don't just take a dirty dish and chunk it in the dishwasher with the food still stuck all over it.
- ✓ You need to load the dishwasher properly. There is a certain logical order of doing this.
- ✓ If you do it wrong, your queen will let you know about it.
- ✓ If you have to wash the dishes anyway, why even use the dishwasher.
- ✓ Women find it sexy to see their husbands standing at the sink washing the dishes by hand. Doing so may lead to some special payback later. So, if I am going to wash dishes anyway, I will choose the old fashion way.
- ✓ Put the remote down.
- ✓ Step away from the recliner.
- ✓ Surprise your sweetheart tonight.
- ✓ Take a load off of her.
- ✓ Treat each day of marriage like the first day.
- ✓ We must keep the romance going.
- ✓ Mix things up and keep your relationship fresh so it doesn't get stuck in a rut.
- ✓ Look for new ways to surprise her.

✓ Read "Song of Songs" and learn some squishy talk like King Solomon used, "How beautiful you are my darling! Oh, how beautiful! Your eyes are doves."

✓ Wash some dishes and quote some Solomon and see what happens.

Sex

The word sex is a small word, and it only has three letters, but it packs a powerful punch. The simple mention of the word sends your mind into a state of overdrive.

Almost everywhere you look these days, you see sex. Advertising agencies use sex all over the place to sell products. You see sex on billboards, in TV commercials, in magazines, in the movies, on the news, in the newspapers, on nightly TV shows, and walking down the street. It is all over. You have probably heard of the term "sex sells." Sex is most likely one of the top sellers in the world. Once again, such a small word, yet it carries a powerful punch.

For some people, the punch is too powerful. For the people who get caught up in the addiction of sex and can't get out of its grip, the results are devastating. Some even lose their life because of it. Some get diseases such as AIDS and die.

Also, there are those who get caught up in affairs and get killed by an angry spouse or significant other. Men who are addicted to pornography can literally lose their wives because of it. I heard another preacher one time say that "Sin will take you farther than you ever intended to go and keep you there longer than you intended to stay and cost you more than you intended to pay." How true this is.

For some men, it may start out as a simple glance at a half-naked woman on a magazine cover at the grocery store. If you only glance and then take that thought captive in the name of Jesus, then that's all right. One can read in the Bible,

> We demolish arguments and every pretension that sets itself up against the knowledge of God, and we take captive every thought to make it obedient to Christ.

2 Corinthians 10:5 (NIV)

However, if your glance turns into a trance and you stay focused on that image all the way home and then that night when you make love to your wife and you're still thinking about the woman on the magazine cover, you are at the beginning of a really bad habit. If you go to the next level, you might pick up a soft porn magazine on the way home from work the next day, thinking to yourself that these pictures are not graphic, it won't hurt anything to look at them; after all they are just models. If you start trying to justify what you are doing and talking yourself into believing that it's all innocent, then you are at stage two of a really bad habit. A good rule of thumb is, if you have to try to justify whether something you are thinking about doing is right or wrong, then it is probably wrong.

Well, here we are at stage two. You have been looking at soft porn for a little while, and you begin to start wondering about maybe purchasing some sex videos.

You say to yourself, "Well this might just teach me a few things that I can try with my wife, so it must be okay to do."

The problem is you watch the videos and not once does your wife enter your mind. But you used her to justify getting the videos.

Remember that Satan is really slick and he will try anything to pull you into a sinful life, knowing full well that in the end the sin will destroy you.

The Bible says, "Be self-controlled and alert, your enemy the devil prowls around like a roaring lion looking for someone to devour" (1 Peter 5:8, NIV).

He will make you think everything is innocent, and your own idea. Don't be fooled. If you have to think twice whether it's wrong or right then once again, it is most likely wrong.

Now things are moving along, and your wife is noticing something different about you. You seem distant and cold towards her. She tries to get close to you, and you pull away. She can't satisfy you anymore because you have allowed pornography to take her place.

The sad thing is the porn doesn't give you near the satisfaction that a loving sexual relationship with your wife does.

You feel guilty and you want to please her, but you are hooked, and your mind is programmed into thinking it needs videos, magazines, and the computer to satisfy its lustful desires.

Before long, your wife is packing up and moving out, and you wind up all alone. You start worrying because you are a Christian, and you hope she hasn't told anyone at the church about your problem.

To fix this situation, you stop going to church all together. Then your life only gets worse. You feel far from God and ashamed. It all started with a glance at a magazine cover. Once again, "Sin will take you farther than you ever intended to go, and keep you there longer than you intended to stay and cost you more than you ever intended to pay.

If this is you, I am truly sorry. I must urge you though to get back in the church. God has the power to heal you from your addictions supernaturally. God will also forgive you and wipe your slate clean.

The Bible says,

> Therefore, there is now no condemnation for those who are in Christ Jesus, because through Christ Jesus the law of the Spirit of life set me free from the law of sin and death.

Romans 8:1 (NIV)

So, if we repent of our sins and turn from the sins and turn to God in Jesus's name, we can put our past behind us and go forward without shame.

Other Christians who are walking righteously will not judge you either; "We have all sinned and fallen short of the glory of God" (Romans 3:23, NIV).

Jesus is standing at the door, waiting for people to invite him into their hearts.

Jesus said,

> Here I am, I stand at the door and knock. If anyone hears my voice and opens the door, I will come in and eat with him and him with me.
>
> Revelation 3:20 (NIV)

He covered our sins on the cross, and he forgives all sins. No matter how badly you think you may have been, there is nothing you have done that God won't forgive you for. But the time to take action is now.

For it is written,

> As God's fellow workers we urge you not to receive God's grace in vain. For He says, 'In the time of my favor I heard you, and in the day of salvation I helped you. I tell you; now is the time of God's favor, now is the day of salvation.
>
> 2 Corinthians 6:1–2 (NIV)

If your wife has left you and you think there is no hope, just remember there is always hope in Jesus Christ. He can change any situation, and if you are willing and you return back to him, he can restore your family.

I have seen family situations where there looked like there was no hope for restoration, completely turned around by prayer and the power of faith in Jesus. God can bring about events that will glue your lives back together. In other words, God can make a way where there is no way.

Paul wrote,

> But since there is so much immorality, each man should have his own wife and each woman her own husband. The husband should fulfill his marital duty to his wife, and likewise the wife to her husband. The wife's body does not belong to her alone but also to her husband. In the same way the husbands' body does not belong to him alone but also to his wife. Do not deprive each other except by mutual consent and for a time, so that you may devote yourselves to prayer. Then come together again so that Satan will not tempt you because of your lack of self- control

1 Corinthians 7:2–5, (NIV)

It is written in the Bible,

> Marriage should be honored by all, and the marriage bed kept pure, for God will judge the adulterer and all the sexually immoral.

Hebrews 13:4 (NIV)

It is clear what God thinks about marriage. He wants us to respect it. Following God's will is the best way to eliminate confusion and trouble in our lives.

Happiness is just around the corner for all who make the choice to follow the Almighty. There is nothing better than a great healthy sexual relationship with one's wife. This is the way God intended it to be and that's why it is the best way to do it. So, put the book down and go tell your wife you love her. Oh, and wash those dishes while you're up. The sparks will be flying before you know it. Have fun and don't be so serious all the time. Take God seriously and your marriage seriously, in a respectful and honorable kind of way, but when it comes to life, we need to find something to smile about, or better yet laugh out loud about. Life is too short to frown. Life goes too quickly to be down.

Points to Ponder

- ✓ The word sex is a small word with only three letters but it packs a very powerful punch.
- ✓ Almost everywhere you look these days you see sex somewhere.
- ✓ Advertising agencies use sex all over the place to sell products.
- ✓ You see sex on billboards, TV commercials, in magazines, in the movies, on the news, in the newspapers, on nightly TV shows, and walking down the street.

- ✓ You have probably heard the term "sex sells."
- ✓ Sex is most likely one of the top sellers in the world. After all, prostitution is called the world's oldest profession.
- ✓ For some people, the punch of this three-letter word is too powerful.
- ✓ For people who get caught up in the addiction of sex and can't get out of its grip, the results are devastating.
- ✓ Some even lose their life because of it.
- ✓ Some get diseases and die.
- ✓ Some get addicted to pornography and lose their wives.
- ✓ "Sin will take you farther than you ever intended to go, and keep you there longer than you ever intended to stay and cost you more than you intended to pay."
- ✓ Addiction starts subtly. It can start with a glance at a scantily clad woman on the cover of a magazine at the grocery store and then lead to a soft porn magazine like *Playboy*, and then to more explicit porn magazines and then to videos, and then the next thing you know, you forget about the woman God gave you, and you start living in a fantasy world that will ultimately destroy you.
- ✓ If you have to try to justify whether or not something is right or wrong, then it is probably wrong.

✓ Satan is slick and he will do anything to pull you into a sinful life.
✓ If you get addicted to pornography, your wife will start noticing a change in you.
✓ It's not too late to turn your life around.
✓ If your wife has already left you and you think there is no hope, remember, with Jesus, there is always hope. Remember that God is a God of restoration.
✓ God can bring about events that will glue your family back together.

Divorce

If you loved her enough to marry her in the first place, then you can love her enough now to stay with her. Too many people are taking the easy way out of their problems these days.

People are trading spouses like they trade in their car every few years. I know this because I am guilty of it. Before I totally sold out to Jesus, I had my priorities all messed up. My philosophy was that if my wife made me mad on a regular basis, I would hang around for a little while, and then I was out the door.

I did not respect marriage enough or God's way enough to try to work things out. I understand that there are many different circumstances that can be involved, and I am in no way naïve about the subject. Marriage is much more serious than a lot of people give it credit for.

If this book keeps just one person from making my mistakes, then it was well worth the effort. It is my prayer that you stick it out even when times are tough because as somebody once said, "Tough times don't last but tough people do."

If you press through the bad times, you will get to smoother waters on the other side, trust me.

What I would like to address are the marriages that are ending over trivial matters, and marriages that are taking place without any thought in the first place about what forever means. Some people meet and say, "You want to get married?" The other person says, "Sure." And there you have it. About a month later, after the sex wears off, they wake up and say, "Who are you and why did we get married?" The other says, "I don't have the foggiest, and by the way, who are you?"

The next thing you know, they are down at the courthouse filing for a divorce. The next night, they are out looking for somebody else to fill up the empty hole left by the last person. I know this sounds crazy but it's true.

When I was younger, I am sorry to admit, I did it myself, shocked, surprised, and amazed. Yes, me—the Christian man who seems so together, so knowledgeable, and so mature.

Well, all I have to say is how do you think I learned all of these lessons? I learned them from the "school of hard knocks." I have messed up so much in my life that I am an authority on many, many things. I definitely know *what not to do*, and I know the agony and the consequences of doing things the wrong way, out of the will of God. Man, have

I learned my lesson. That is why I am writing this book because I don't want anyone else to suffer like I have from my own stupidity.

Please listen to what I have to say because you do not want to go through what I have gone through. I am here to say that when you turn your back on God, he will let you get away with stuff for a long time. So long even that you may think that you are going to get away free and clean, but let me tell you that there will come a day when he will say *enough!*

If you have already been saved like I had when I was fifteen, then you are held more accountable than those who are not saved. Then you can't get away with anything. If you get out of God's will after you have been saved, you can't throw a piece of gum wrapper out of the car window without getting caught.

God disciplines his children, which is actually a good thing. The Word of God says, "Stern discipline awaits him who leaves the path" (Proverbs 15:10, NIV).

Finally, after years of backsliding and turning from God, I have turned back around, and life is much better now. I have a lovely wife of twelve years, and now that I have approached marriage from God's perspective, it has made things so much better.

We still fight and argue; she still gets on my nerves and I get on her nerves. There are times when we can't seem to stand each other. Nothing has changed marriage-wise from before, except that when God is in charge and in control, we don't let a fight or our anger lead to thoughts of divorce.

Even if we threaten to leave each other, we know that we are not serious. No matter what we say, at the end of most arguments, we usually wind up laughing at how silly we look. Most of the time, we are fighting over something ridiculously trivial.

Five minutes after a fight with my wife now, we just go on talking as if there was never a harsh word said, like nothing happened.

This is different from before because when I used to get into a fight with my wife, I would stay mad for up to a month at a time.

We would go weeks without speaking with one another. There was no peace in the house, nothing but turmoil.

Without putting the Lord first in your marriage, there will be no true peace. But if you put the Lord first, he will put a spirit of peace in your home. Take strength in the Lord. Nehemiah said, "Do not grieve, for the joy of the Lord is your strength" (Nehemiah 8:10, NIV).

The Bible tells us, "In your anger do not sin. Do not let the sun go down while you are still angry, and do not give the devil a foothold" (Ephesians 4:26–27, NIV). If you let the devil get his foot in the door, sooner or later he will get all the way into your home and have you right where he wants you.

A home full of peace is good for everyone. It is good for the husband and wife. It is good for the children. Peace is even good for the pets. When people come to visit, they will be able to feel the peace in the home.

Jesus said,

> I have told you these things, so that in me you may have peace. In this world you will have trouble. But take heart! I have overcome the world.
>
> John 16:33 (NIV)

I believe that when all else fails, Jesus doesn't. I believe that with God, "All things are possible" (Matthew 19:26, NIV). I believe that in order to make a wife happy, all it takes is two ingredients—Jesus and the husband. When one adds these two ingredients together, one can say, "I can do everything through him who gives me strength" (Philippians 4:13, NIV).

Points to Ponder

✓ If you loved her enough to marry her in the first place, then you can love her enough now to stay with her.

✓ Too many people are taking the easy way out of their problems these days.

✓ People are trading their spouses like they trade in their cars every few years.

- ✓ Don't get married without giving serious thought to what forever means.
- ✓ Arguments occur in all marriages. Two people are never going to agree on everything. Just don't let your fights and anger lead to thoughts of divorce.
- ✓ Do not hold on to your anger after an argument. Just forget it and move on. It is not worth it and God does not want us to "let the sun go down on our anger" (Ephesians 4:26–27, NIV).
- ✓ Without putting the Lord first in your marriage, there will be no true peace. But if you put the Lord first, he will put a spirit of peace in your home.
- ✓ "The joy of the Lord is your strength" (Nehemiah 8:10, NIV).
- ✓ Jesus plus the husband equal a happy wife.

Communication

If you don't effectively communicate with your spouse, your relationship will go south. I speak from experience. I am a soldier who has spent a great deal of time away from my wife, over in the big Iraqi sandbox. Then because of an injury on the battlefield and a small issue with cancer, I had to spend yet another great deal of time away from my wife in an army hospital in San Antonio, Texas. Each time I went away, it seemed harder to return.

When you are away from your spouse for a long time and your communication is cut off, you tend to become strangers to one another. I realize this is the worst case scenario, but it can also apply to a couple who actually live together but for some reason after some time has passed after the honeymoon, they quit talking. The spark goes out, the flame goes out, the fire goes out, you have to turn on the oven just to generate some heat in the house.

Why does this happen? Why do our flames go out? It seems to happen to most couples. How can we work through these tough times? I wrote a song about a relationship, and the words go like this,

> When I met her I could do no wrong, and neither could she. We were two little love birds sitting in a big old tree. Now some time has passed and I'm looking for a place to rent. Because her getup and love, got up and went. She used to let me hold her tight and look into her eyes. And whisper sweet nothings that I thought were pretty wise. Now she won't give me the time of day all her love is spent. Yes her getup and love got up and went.

Does this relationship sound familiar? The words to this song came so easily to me. It seems that this is the way it goes with a lot of relationships. They start out great. Both people are head over hills goofy and blind to all the little imperfections of the other person. They don't notice on the first twenty dates that their partner smacks and eats with food in his mouth. Or his partner licks her fingers after she eats a bite of greasy ribs or chicken. It's all good. Burping is good, passing gas is good, picking the nose is good—it is all good.

However, if you live with anyone long enough, nerves will become tender. It will be just like somebody jaywalking in Mayberry. Your chest will stick out, the blood vessels will pop out of your forehead, the muscles in your neck will tighten, and you will flat freak out. There will come a point in time when you will not be able to stand your partner's bad habits any longer.

You are probably asking yourselves and me right now what in the heck would be the appropriate way to handle this situation. I can easily tell you what doesn't work because I have tried several different things. I have suffered the consequences too. I guess the best way to handle these situations is when you see your spouse doing something that really bothers you, like licking all four fingers and a thumb after chomping down a rack of ribs, you should say nothing until you leave the dining facility.

There is nothing worse than making a scene in a public place. And believe me you will mention it quietly to her, but the scene I am talking about is her response to your comment. She is the one who will embarrass you by talking loud enough for everyone to hear how you just insulted her in public.

When you get in your car to drive to the movies, you might very nicely say, "You know honey, I am sure you have been doing this all of your life, and it is really not a huge deal, but it kind of bothers me when you lick your fingers at the table when we are out in public. Now if you must do it, and there is no other way then fine, but I am asking you to please, if you could, refrain from doing so, in public, and if there is something that I do that bothers you, please feel free to tell me and I will do my best to honor your wishes for me to stop."

Somebody once said that, "You catch more flies with honey." I think that if you take the soft approach, you are less likely to get a negative response, your spouse will be more likely to honor your wishes.

Maybe she won't, but you will feel better either way for getting the issue off of your chest and this is very important to a lasting relationship because we don't want to keep things bottled up inside of us, because if we do, it can cause health problems.

Another thing that can happen when we keep things bottled up inside is that if we do get mad and have an argument with our spouse at some point in time which most of us, if not all of us do from time to time, then all of the things that we have bottled up inside tend to all come out of us at once, and we say things that are very hurtful to our loved ones, and this can sometimes cause permanent damage.

Somebody said that a tornado only takes about thirty seconds to plow through a home, but the damage it leaves can last a lifetime. This is what can happen when we blow up and say harmful things to our wives. It may only take a few seconds of yelling to cut her down before we calm down and get over it, but the damage that it caused may last a lifetime. We need to try to control our words even when we get upset, so that we don't say things that we'll regret.

To sum it up, remember to communicate your feelings with your spouse. You don't have to be away at war to drift apart in your relationship. You can become strangers in your own home. Don't let this happen, be inquisitive, ask your wife every day how her day was, and tell her how your day was.

When your wife is talking to you, look at her, and let her know you are listening. My wife gets really disappointed when I appear to not be paying attention to her when she is speaking to me, even if I am hearing what she is saying. It shows her that you respect her when you take a few minutes to turn the television down, or put the newspaper down, and give her your undivided attention.

If your wife is doing something that bothers you, like licking her fingers in public, remember to watch how you go about telling her. Don't do it in public, wait until you get to the car or home. Remember the saying, "You catch more flies with honey." Don't keep things bottled up because what is bottled up usually tends to blow up eventually, which can cause permanent damage or a trip down town.

Also it has been said that, "A family that plays together, stays together." Playing board games at home offer a great way to spend fun one-on-one time with your wife, and it allows for general conversation that is not heavy or stressful.

There is a saying that is perhaps more important though and that is, "A family that prays together, stays together." A family that puts God first, family second, and then their job third are more likely to stay together than a family that doesn't acknowledge God.

There is a peace that only a relationship with God's Son can give. People who do not know Jesus have emptiness about them. A great number of people try to fill that emptiness with alcohol, drugs, sex, gambling, and a host of other things that lead to a path of destruction.

I can tell you from experience that no amount alcohol can fill the void. No amount of material wealth and possessions can fill the hole, only Jesus can.

Speaking of communication, we should communicate with God constantly through prayer. He will watch over us, and put a hedge of protection over us, and our family, and yes even our marriages. It wasn't until I completely surrendered my life to Jesus that I could stay married. I have been married a few times before I met my current wife, and the reason that I did not stay married was because I lacked in all the areas that I am writing about.

I am putting in this book the lessons I learned from the wrong things I had done in the past. Sure it wasn't my entire fault, but I must take the blame for some of it because there are two sides to every story. The single biggest mistake that I made in the past is that I did not put God first. I did not consult with God and ask him how I should handle situations. I did not even ask God if those I have been with were the right people.

I was trying to make all of my decisions on my own, and I have found that you just cannot do that.

A life without God's wisdom is a life destined for failure. It may not happen overnight, but believe me, it will happen. It wasn't until I surrendered all to Jesus my precious savior that my life finally reached a peace on earth.

Points to Ponder

- ✓ If you don't communicate effectively with your spouse, your relationship will go south.
- ✓ When a lot of people meet, they don't notice each other's imperfections. They are just head over heels goofy for one another. However, after the physical attraction wears off, then the irritants begin.
- ✓ What you have to do is keep the lines of communication open and let each other *respectfully* know what you're thinking.
- ✓ Don't make a scene in public.
- ✓ Use kind and gentle words to let your spouse know what is going on in your head. However you need to be honest. Either that or just learn to accept your wife's behavior.
- ✓ It is possible to accept certain things. In fact, there are certain things in life that we have to accept whether we like them or not.
- ✓ We also need to realize that our wives have probably learned to accept a great deal of things that we as men do that they can't stand. Need I go into detail?

- ✓ If you take the soft approach, you are less likely to get a negative response.
- ✓ Ask your wife daily how her day was.
- ✓ When she is describing it, don't ignore her, focus on what she is saying.
- ✓ A family that prays together stays together.
- ✓ Families need to include Jesus to have peace.
- ✓ There is a peace that only Jesus can give.
- ✓ A great number of people use alcohol, gambling, drugs, and a host of other things to try to find peace and happiness.
- ✓ These other methods do not fill any gaps. They just create bigger gaps, and lead down a path to destruction.
- ✓ We should also communicate with God constantly through prayer.
- ✓ It is a good idea to go to God in prayer before you make important decisions in your life. He will let you know if what you are planning is right or wrong. We must open our spiritual ears and listen to his will so we will learn in time to know what is right as we go through listening to his voice.
- ✓ A life without God's wisdom is a life destined for failure.
- ✓ It wasn't until I surrendered all to Jesus my precious savior that my life finally reached a peace on earth.

You Don't Send Me Flowers Anymore

You don't send me flowers anymore is something that should never be heard coming from the mouth of your wife. That is if you are truly interested in having your best wife now. You would simply be amazed at how much happiness, self-esteem, and confirmation of love can come from a bouquet of flowers.

My wife worked with a lot of other women, and when a woman got flowers where she worked, whoever received the flowers would parade around with them showing off saying, "Look what my 'hubby' got me, look what my hubby got me." This infuriated the other women. They all put on a fake smile and said, "Oh how nice," when they were really thinking, *Just who does she think she is, prancing around showing off her flowers like some floozy!* Then an atomic explosion would go off in their brain, and guess who the target would be? You guessed it, their husband.

So if you have a wife that works in a building with a bunch of other women, I think I would be running to the nearest flower shop about now because you don't know who else might be reading this book. And if you have any friends that you really care about, you might want to purchase them a copy of this book just to help save their lives, I mean marriages.

I can guarantee you that if another woman gets flowers at work today, you will get the you-don't-send-me-flowers-any-more speech when you get home—that is, if you have not sent your wife flowers lately. If you have, then remind your friends to do so because I have been through this speech, and believe me, when it was over, I felt so low that I could walk under a snakes belly and not even have to duck.

If you are not into buying flowers, that's all right because there are plenty of other things you can do to keep you out of the dog house and off of the couch.

For instance, you can take your wife to a fancy dinner one night a week and call it a date night. You can write love notes, and place them all over the house and in the car where you know your wife will find them, and not your housekeeper. That could be a whole other book right there.

There might be a tiny bit of confusion going on if the housekeeper was making the bed and found a note under the pillow that said, "Meet me at the Grand Hotel for a special evening of love room 222." Think of the look on your face when you answer the door in your Scooby–Doo boxers, and find the housekeeper standing there in fishnet stockings and a miniskirt. What a nightmare huh? Be careful where you put the notes. Don't put them where the kids can find them, it might confuse them. They might lose all their faith in the Storks.

Just be creative and you will find that things will start improving in your relationship. Tell your wife that you love her and that she is beautiful. And if she asks you if a dress makes her look fat, don't say yes; come on men, I've actually heard of men who say yes. Yes is not the right answer, the answer is, "Darling, I don't care about the dress or how it looks, or how it makes you look, all that I know is that what is inside the dress lives the most beautiful and sexy woman I have ever seen." That is what you tell the woman you love.

We live in a world of sin, but we don't have to be of this world. If we are followers of Jesus, we are born again and dead to the sin of the world. The Bible says, "Dear friends, I urge you, as aliens and strangers in the world, to abstain from sinful desires, which war against your soul" (1 Peter 2:11, NIV).

Being that, we have Christ Jesus in our lives, we can have successful marriages because we are no longer of this world so to speak. We are the salt of the earth and we are to let Jesus be seen in us because it may be that for some, the only Jesus they will see is the Jesus in you and in me.

We must let him shine through for "he is the way, the truth and the life" (John 14:6, NIV). When we bring his peace to our marriages, there is an automatic benefit and blessing upon them. If we keep his peace in our marriages and follow God's commands, then the chances that we will ever get a divorce becomes dimmer and dimmer by the day until they slowly fade out of sight.

I think it is the most exciting thing in the world to experience marriage, love, and closeness the way God intended it to be. For God designed it to be perfect, and when we deviate from his way and do things our way, we immediately feel the weight of our imperfections bearing down upon us. And the more we deviate, the heavier the weight gets, and it will get heavier and heavier, until we cannot hold it up any longer, and it is at these points where relationships fail.

It is at these points where health declines. After all, "the wages of sin is death" (Romans 6:23). We can choose to live in a nightmare, or in a world filled with happiness, rest, peace, and fulfillment. "We can choose the broad path that leads to destruction, or the narrow path that leads to life everlasting" (Matthew 7:13, NIV). We can stop and buy the roses because when we change our hearts for God, he changes our hearts for good. He changes our hearts to do the good things that promote great marriages. God is love.

Points to Ponder

✓ "You don't send me flowers anymore" is something that should never be heard from the mouth of your wife.

✓ Flowers can boost your wife's self-esteem. They let your wife know that she is worth something to you, they bring her happiness, and they let her know she is loved.

✓ If your wife works around a lot of other women, then sending flowers is a must. If the other wives are getting flowers at work, and your wife is not, then she will feel a great deal of hurt. On the other hand, if your wife is getting flowers and the other ladies are not, then she will be flocked around and the ladies will be asking her where she found such a sweet husband. Flowers are more important than you might think.

✓ If you have not purchased flowers for your wife lately, then now is a good time.

✓ If you have, well I am proud of you sir, and I respectfully ask that you suggest to a friend to do the same.

✓ If you are not into flowers, then you can take your wife to dinner maybe once a week and call it date night.

✓ Perhaps you can write love notes to your wife and place them around the house or in your vehicle where you know your wife, and not the maid will find them.

✓ Heck, if you can't afford flowers, get her a card that says, "Honey, I love you, and you are the most important person on earth to me."

✓ Be creative and try different things. Don't get too weird like the man I used to work with did. His wife had complained he was not being spontaneous enough. He cooked dinner one evening and stripped down, painted his body purple, and glued horns on top of his bald head. When his wife got home from work, she walked in the door, and he said "Surprise honey, I cooked dinner, is this spontaneous enough for you?" His wife left him and never returned. So be careful not to go too far.

✓ When we bring the peace of the Lord Jesus to our marriages, there is an automatic blessing upon them. When we are obedient to the word of God and we love and take care of our wives, then God will honor that obedience and make a peaceful home. If we are in his will, then our home lives will be all that God intended them to be. It is when we get out of alignment that we get into trouble with our families.

✓ "A compliment a day keeps divorce far, far away."

✓ When we change our hearts for God, he changes our hearts for good.

Don't Stress Me Out!

As you well know, we live in a very stressful world today. Stress can put a damper on a relationship quicker than bunny rabbits can make babies. That is not long considering that when we get married, we make a commitment for life. I am by no means a psychiatrist, and I don't pretend to be an expert on stress. I just know that I have been through a lot of it, and it has taken a huge toll on me. It has also put stress on my relationship.

You see, even the strongest of relationships are not impervious to the dreadful attack of the stress monster. It can turn the best of lovers into the coldest of ice cubes, if not carefully monitored and without a continuous bleeding of the pressure valves.

Everyone is unique, and people have different ways of releasing their stresses. The most important thing about letting off steam is not to destroy anything in the process. Find a way to let it out in such a way that the television does not get shot, or the glass of tea you are drinking doesn't smash through a window as it swishes past your spouse's head.

Now we must realize that a spouse can make us madder than anybody else on earth. There is nobody who can make us more mad than our spouse. Everyone that is married has had some disagreements, and the disagreements are usually regulated by the amount of stress we are under at the particular time of the hostility.

Now let's talk about stress itself. It has been said that 75–90 percent of all visits to a primary care physician's office are related to stress disorders. People are on all sorts of medications to alleviate their stress. The problem is the medications come with side effects that are worse than the cure. So what are we to do?

First, I would pray for healing from the effects of stress on your life. Then I would be sure to seek help from a medical professional if the stress becomes overwhelming. There are certified Christian counselors that you can go to as well.

I try to use humor when I am in a stressful environment. When I was a soldier in Iraq, I had to stay upbeat, and keep things as light and funny as possible. I would joke around with the Iraqi people and try to put them at ease, to let them know that we were not there to harm them but to help them rebuild their country, and live as free people. When we had to search their homes for insurgents, weapons, and stolen property, I could see the stress in the faces of the women and children, and my heart hurt for them. I tried to put myself in their shoes and asked myself how I would feel if an army from another nation was coming into my home and digging through my personal stuff.

I tried to imagine what fear the children might be feeling because they had been told all of their lives that Americans are evil, and we killed innocent people.

They must have been terrified, and I am sorry that we had to do what we did. It was necessary though. Even in the midst of the most stressful of times, humor can go a long way to put people at ease. It is an instant stress relief valve that can be used at any time.

This technique can be used in your relationship too. If life starts getting too heavy for you and the stress monster pays a visit, pull out a joke book and start reading. Turn on a DVD of your favorite comedian. Find a comedy on television. Read a funny book. Find something fun to do to get your mind off of your worries before your worries build up to an unmanageable degree. Because all too often, we tend to let our stresses out on the persons we care about the most, and that is our wives.

There is a saying that, "The new husband soon learns that his bride may be too cute for words but not for arguments." Another saying goes, "Life is 10 percent what you make it and 90 percent how you take it."

How we take what happens to us is so important. It is actually something we do have control over. We may not be able to change our life's circumstances, but we can change how we react to them. We can choose to be positive and keep our chin up with a smile on our face. Or we can choose to hang our heads low and walk around with a frown on our faces. It's up to us how we react. Isn't that great? It makes me want to jump up and down with joy.

A simple smile can change the atmosphere all around us. We can actually influence a whole set of events just with a simple smile and a greeting. Life is too short to be down and out. Don't let the troubles of life get the better of you. You have the power within you to stop this wretchedness in its tracks.

So what do you say? Are you going to work on stressing less? I know that you can do it and that your relationship will see great improvement.

You've heard the saying, "If Momma ain't happy ain't nobody happy, if Daddy ain't happy ain't nobody cares." I know it doesn't sound fair, but as the great marriage counselors of today say, "You can be right or you can be happy."

Let her be right, and you will sleep tight. Let her be right, and life will be out of sight. Let her be right and life will be dynamite! Who remembers J.J. Walker? No, I am not talking about Walker Texas Ranger; J.J. Walker from television's *Good Times*. I loved that show.

This concludes my chapter on stress. I hope it was helpful to you. Like I said, I don't have a degree in psychology, but

I have been through the school of hard knocks. I have a lot of experience being married, and I know what works, and what gets you put in the dog house. Yes, I have been in the dog house plenty of times. In fact, I have been there so often that I had to purchase a flea collar. I even know how to roll over and play dead, and let me tell you, this one comes in handy sometimes. You might call it a defense mechanism. I am sure that you will do just fine.

Don't worry about a thing. Life is not always going to be a bed of roses, but it doesn't have to stink. Remember that you carry the air freshener in your mind. You can spray whatever fragrance that you want to on it.

Points to Ponder

✓ Stress can put a damper on a relationship rather quickly.

✓ I have experienced a great deal of stress in my life and boy has it taken its toll on me and my relationships.

✓ Even the strongest relationships are not impervious to the stress monster.

✓ We should not let our stress build up. However, we should find ways to release it that are safe and that are not destructive. In other words don't shoot the television set, or don't throw a glass of tea at the wall narrowly missing you wife's head.

✓ Realize that there will be times when your wife will make you really mad, and there will be times when you make her really mad. If this happens, maybe you will want to separate for a couple of hours and pray about it and ask God to calm the situation down. Just try not to break anything in your anger, especially one another's hearts.

✓ About 75–90 percent of all visits to primary health care providers are caused by stress disorders.

✓ There are a lot of ways to deal with stress. I choose my belief in God and my Savior his son Jesus, and a heavy dose of humor. The Bible says that, "Laughter is good medicine"

✓ (Proverbs 17:22, NIV).

✓ Find something that you and your wife can laugh at.

✓ There is a saying, "Life is 10 percent what you make it and 90 percent how you take it." Please apply this to your marriage.

✓ Life is not always a bed of roses but it doesn't have to stink.

✓ You carry the air freshener in your mind and you can spray whatever fragrance you want to into your life.

Blended Families

If you've married someone who already had children, and you already had children as well at the time, then this chapter is a must read. You may have already solved all of the challenges in your blended family, and if you have, my hat is off to you because I know it was a bumpy road to travel.

However, if you have only been married a short time, and your blended family life is a nightmare on your street, then my heart goes out to you. Fear not though for it will get better.

I am on my twelfth year of a blended family marriage and it took a while for things to smooth out. When I married my wife, she had three daughters—the youngest was about six years old, the middle child was about fifteen years old, and the oldest was about twenty years old. I had a five-year-old daughter that I was bringing into the marriage.

My wife and I discussed the situation before we got married, and we acknowledged that there would probably be some difficulties in blending these kids together, especially with the fifteen-year-old, having a male authority figure coming into the home changed the way she was used to living, which was pretty much doing her own thing and helping her mother raise the six-year-old while she was away at work.

My kid did not like having another Mom and another authority figure in her life either. So she would tell her mother during visitation times that my wife was mean to her, and this news reached all the way to my ex-mother-in-law. My ex-mother-in-law wrote me a very nasty letter expressing her displeasure with me allowing this mean woman to treat her grandbaby badly. Of course this would upset my wife, and I wound up having an upset wife, an upset ex-wife, an upset ex-mother-in-law, and two upset daughters right off the bat.

They all wanted me to fix the problem. I was between a rock and a hard place. I called my ex-mother-in-law, and told her that my wife was not mistreating my daughter, and I did not appreciate the accusations.

The next thing you know, my ex-wife was taking me to court to try to take custody of my daughter while telling the court that my daughter was in an abusive situation.

If ever I wanted to crawl in a hole and disappear, this was the time. There was no way for me to please everyone. I was totally distraught and did not know what I was supposed to do about the situation. The only thing I knew to do at the time was to pray to God that he would take control of the situation, and I just let go—I "let go, and let God" (Psalm 46:10, NIV).

This calmed me down. My wife was hurt because she was being accused of these horrible things, and like me, there was nothing she could do about it but pray. I will say that praying helped a great deal.

Another thing my wife and I did was go to a bookstore and purchased a book on blended families. It helped to read a book written by someone who had been there and done that. The only people who can truly understand a blended family nightmare are people who have experienced it, and lived through to tell about it. These people understand your dilemma.

I am one of these people, and I am going to share some of my experiences and tell you how we handled them. Then you can apply what you read about my family to your situation, and hopefully after some time and patience, you will get through the bumpy roads which we all face at the beginning, and things will smooth out into a peaceful flow.

I will start with the youngest daughters and work my way up. As I mentioned earlier, my daughter was about five and my wife's daughter was about six. First of all, my daughter was used to having my undivided attention and having to share that attention with my wife was very hard for her to swallow.

She became withdrawn and appeared to be depressed because she did not have the access that she once had. Now this broke my heart because I was very close to her. She was my pride and joy. I had trouble not just telling my wife that I'm sorry, but I have to give my time to my kiddo. When I would mention how I felt about not spending time with my kid, my wife would sometimes get upset thinking that my kid was playing a game just to steal my time away from her and the kids did play these games to put us on guilt trips and they worked for a long time.

But at the same time, they do need attention. As a parent in this situation, we need to find a way to balance our time so that the children get a healthy portion of our attention. We just can't give them all of our time though because this will destroy our marriages.

Perhaps one could schedule his time so that the kids get certain blocks of time and the wife gets certain blocks of time, and most importantly, God gets certain blocks of time. It should go in this order: God, wife, and kids.

Now I will go to the next daughter who is biologically my wife's and was about six years old. When my wife and I were married, the six-year-old would have a tendency to be clingy to her mother. She had been used to getting her mother's undivided attention. When I came along, I messed all of that up. She had a way of making her mom feel guilty to try to take her mother away from me when we would try to share some quiet time together. This would upset me, and I would accuse the young one of playing a game to keep her mother and me apart.

These two were used to being the center of attention, so naturally they clashed when they came together and had to learn to share for the first time. They would mess with each other, and then come and tell on one another, always trying to get the other one in trouble. This also caused trouble with me and my wife because I would take my daughter's side and she would take her daughter's side. We would really get into some really bad arguments over these things. The six-year-old is now twenty, and I have adopted her. Adopting her has really helped to bring peace to our home.

Then there was the fifteen-year-old. She would say things like, "He is not my father; he is just a man who married my mother." She really resented me for a while. Her best friend had a stepfather, and she had convinced my daughter that all stepfathers were bad. She had her mind made up that I was bad, and nothing in the immediate future was going to change that. This did not ease any of the blended family tension that was in the air.

She now has a good job and a nice home. We now have a great relationship. I believe that if a blended family can make it through the first four or five years, things will smooth out and come together. You have to remember that children, who are thrust into a new family, are most often still trying to get over the pain of losing their previous family. And even though the previous family life was packed full of fighting and screaming, and may have been totally abusive, children do not want their parents to separate. They put themselves into a state of denial, and they choose to remember only the good times and block out the painful times.

I am a child of divorced parents and when my dad would bring home a girlfriend, I immediately resented her, and if she had children, I resented them too. I wanted things to go back to the way they were.

What children do is try to destroy the blended family in the hopes that mom and dad will reunite. After several years of living in the new family, those tendencies tend to start fading away, and the children begin to accept the new family as the norm. When they realize that it looks permanent, they begin to relax and feel more secure. So, if you married a woman with kids, and you have kids, just hang in there. I know it sounds impossible to endure several years of adjustment, and sometimes I am sure things happen faster, but you can do it!

Now the twenty-year-old moved out before I moved in. She has never been opposed to or caused any trouble in our relationship. She was married shortly thereafter, and just watched the whole thing from the sidelines. She has always been good to us.

I must admit that there was so much turmoil during the first few years of our marriage that I really had my doubts as to whether or not we could make it through the storm. All that I can say is that God is a God of restoration. I would also like to say that when you fight, and you will fight, try not to hurt your partner during the fight, try to fight fair.

There are certain areas when you fight with a spouse whom you love that you need to stay away from. Don't say anything during your anger that will leave permanent damage to the relationship. It is alright to say what is bothering you, in fact this is healthy but try not to go over the line and say something so hurtful, that it will always linger the rest of your days. I know I have already mentioned this, but it is important enough to repeat over and over.

Just stay after the kids and let them know that you love them, and that it does not matter whether they are step or not; that as far as you are concerned, they are your children and they are a gift from God. It is good to get the children to communicate their feelings to each other and to their parents so they can feel like they are being heard and understood. They will feel important and like they count for something in the family. We choose not to use the word step in our family by the way. I am using it for the purposes of this book, but we don't use it at home. We do not hold any resentment toward any of the kids for any troublesome actions because we realize that their actions were normal and directly related to their circumstances.

In all the cases I have read or heard about, it takes about five years for things to normalize. It is a gradual progression. If you think about it things really start to improve as soon as the first family member acts out and lets his or her feelings known.

This is because people become aware of the problem and they can start to work on a solution. After all, you can't fix something until you know it is broken. It will take a long time to fix all of the problems, but the sooner you get started, the sooner you can get out of the rough seas and into the calmer waters.

Blending a family is not an easy task. It is not for the faint of heart. It takes a lot of work and a long time to make things smooth.

There will be times when you will want to give up, and there will be times when you will wonder if it is all worth it. Don't give up, you can make it. It will be worth it.

Remember that the kids will grow up one day and move away. Then it will be just you and your wife. You will probably miss having the kids around. However, if you give up early and divorce, you won't get to spend that time with your wife that only comes when the kids move out.

If you hang in there, then they will bring your grandchildren over to see you, and you will be so proud you stuck it out. You will be grinning from ear to ear. Come on, admit it, you know you will.

So pray, communicate, negotiate, appreciate, don't hesitate, try to relate, try to create, don't speculate, approximate, love your mate, don't be late, have a V-8, fill your plate be glad you ate, go on a date, life will be great, and play crazy eights.

In conclusion to this chapter, I would like to point out the rewards of sticking it out until the waters have had a chance to calm down into a sea of tranquility.

Our blended family has now become one unit to the point where you can no longer see the lines. The scars are smoothing over at the seams. We refer to ourselves as father, mother, and daughters. There is no mention of *step* anymore. We are a real family and we love one another and care for one another in ways that biological families do.

I was also blessed with the opportunity to walk the oldest daughter down the aisle. She is a wonderful mother of two beautiful girls, and she is married to a Christian man who is very involved in their church. He is a pastor and plays guitar and sings praise and worship music. My daughter is involved as well, and she and my son-in-law are both youth ministers. They have a special place in God's heart, and mine as well.

The next daughter, age wise, is now working at a good job, and she visits us often. She helps out around the house when we need extra help. She has bonded with me, and our family is better off with her being a part of it.

The next daughter is now twenty, she is always the comedian. She is attending college in Austin, Texas. She is training to be a school teacher. She went from being the baby of the family to being kind of the middle child. This was not so easy. She is used to it now. It is no big deal.

The youngest daughter is about to turn nineteen. She is the artist of the family. She likes to draw. She went from being an only child to the youngest of four girls. This was quite an adjustment, but she has adapted very well and has learned how to share her love with all of us.

She is a fun loving person, who is very outgoing, and my wife has taught her a great deal of things about life—how to cook, crochet, do homework, etc. My wife has taught her values that involve work ethic and the importance of being responsible, and following through with obligations. She is such a pleasant young lady, she has learned about God and I am glad to be her dad. She is a senior in high school, and she has joined the U.S. Army and has been assigned the job of a military police officer.

In the same way, I have instilled a lot of values into the twenty-year-old who has needed a father figure around and has needed an example of a functional marriage between a husband and wife. Kids need a parent of each gender. A lot of a girl's self-esteem is built up by her father. When I say father, I mean the man who has devoted his life, love, time, and energy to raise her. Almost any man can produce a baby, but not all men who have babies are fathers.

God is truly a God of restoration. He has taken what started out as a bumpy, rough, hard, scary road and transformed it into a picture of peace and tranquility. Our God is an awesome God, Amen.

Points to Ponder

✓ If you have just married a woman who has kids already and you have kids too then I will be honest with you. You need to have honest discussions with your wife that the road that you are on is going to get bumpy.

- ✓ There will be times when you will want to take your kids, turn the car around and charge off in the opposite direction, and there will be times like this for your wife.

- ✓ I must say that over the past twelve years or so, my wife and I have had some really tough times dealing with our blended family. If we had not been open about it from the get–go, we probably would not be married today. It takes honesty and openness on the parent's part to get through the difficult times. I can assure you the kids will not have a problem at all being brutally honest.

- ✓ It will take patience because the kids will try to play you against your wife and her kids will try to get her mad at you, and the kids are very good at what they do. It's just that as the adult, you have to become better at detecting what is really going on in order to stop a problem before it starts.

- ✓ After a couple of years, you will have figured out most of the tricks that the kids will try to play on your mind.

- ✓ Sadly, they can still cause a fight between you and your wife even though you know good and well what they are doing to instigate it.

✓ After four or five years though, you will have mastered not only the games they play, but your own ability to ignore the games, and know when something is real and when something is fake.

✓ Some people would imagine that it is hard enough getting divorced and starting a new relationship with a new spouse, much less try to handle one with ready-made children. I can say that it is not for the faint of heart. You really have to be committed to making it work.

✓ I have found that sometimes running away from a perceived problem is not always the best solution. It is much more rewarding in the end, if you choose to fight through a challenge, and see what a mighty work God can do when you just follow his commands.

✓ God is truly a God of restoration.

The Stepparent Stigma

I believe that stepparents get a bad rap in this world. Just because a person is a stepfather or a stepmother does not automatically make this person a monster.

Granted, I believe that some stepparents are monsters but clearly, so are some biological parents. When a couple enters into a marriage where there are children from another parent, he or she is making a conscious decision to take responsibility for the children.

If a couple has a clear and thorough communicative process before the marriage transpires, and they admit to one another that it won't be an easy road ahead and they devise ways to deal with preconceived scenarios that could arise, then no one should dispute the genuine validity of the stepparent's motives.

It is about being honest with your "spouse-to-be" letting her know that it might not be easy to automatically fall in love with her kids right away but that you love her dearly and that your love for her kids will naturally grow with time.

You have to be honest and admit that at first you will probably get a little upset the first time your new wife disciplines your biological child, and she will most likely get upset when you discipline her child. This is natural at first but it is something that you must get over.

The success of your marriage will hinge strongly upon whether or not you can back your spouse when she is correcting your kid. And she will need to back you when you are correcting her kid.

I will tell you that this was a huge issue at first, even though my wife and I knew it would be before we even got married but it happened anyway. It was our honesty with each other that helped us overcome this issue. We fought over the kids a lot at first.

It may be unpleasant to argue and fight with your spouse over various issues, but as long as it does not get physical and you don't go to bed mad, it is vitally important to the health of your marriage to get the issues resolved as they come.

If you hold your feelings in and avoid confronting the issues that you feel strongly about, but won't share them with your spouse because you are afraid she will get mad at you and want to argue and fight over it, you are treading in dangerous waters.

You see, your feelings will always come out sooner or later. What you want is sooner. If you hold it in, what will happen is you will begin to store your feelings up in the back of your mind and in the pit of your stomach. Holding feelings in is not healthy. If I mention this more than once, it is because I don't want you to forget it.

The best way to handle bothersome issues in a marriage is to handle the issues while they are small enough to manage without having to call in the Po-Po.

My wife and I have never had a problem with just blurting out how we feel. This way we take care of issues as we go. We get upset, argue for a few minutes, then start laughing because we usually forget what we were arguing about, and the kids start laughing with us, or at us, and no one gets scared anymore, and it's all good. Remember not to say mean and hurtful things in the argument that will leave a lasting damage. Stick to the issue at hand.

This takes time to master, especially if you come from a family who never argued, but just held it all in.

Now I know that Jesus said to turn the other cheek, but he was not afraid to confront people when they were out of line. Please get your bible and read Matthew 23:1–36. In this chapter, my Lord Jesus denounced religious hypocrites. He got on to the scribes and Pharisees. He called them snakes and broods of vipers, and hypocrites. He was not happy with them, and he let them know it.

I would like to point out though that when dealing with your wife—the woman that you love—using words like snake, or viper might be a bit too harsh. We are to love our wives like Christ loved the church remember? The whole point I am trying to make is that it is good to speak your mind, and get things talked out as you go, before they get to the point where you are calling your sweetheart a snake.

Here is a great teaching from the Bible in the New Testament,

> Therefore, as God's chosen people, holy and dearly loved, clothe yourselves with compassion, kindness, humility, gentleness and patience; bear with each other and forgive whatever grievances you may have against one another. Forgive as the Lord forgave you. And over all these virtues put on love, which binds them all together in perfect unity. Let the peace of Christ rule in your hearts since as members of one body you were called to peace. And be thankful. Let the word of Christ dwell in you richly as you teach and admonish one another with all wisdom, and as you sing psalms, hymns and spiritual songs with gratitude in your hearts to God. And whatever you do, whether in word or deed, do it all in the name of the Lord Jesus, giving thanks to God the Father through him.
>
> Colossians 3:12–17 (NIV)

Now there is a verse in the above scripture that talks about admonishing one another with all wisdom. The word admonish means to scold gently, or to advise a person about his faults or her faults, or warn against something in order that he or she may be guided to improve.

Using this definition along with God's word, we are able to get a better understanding of how to approach our queens when we have a particular problem or issue that we feel an urgent need to share.

What we find is that we don't want to keep our issues bottled up, and we don't want to call our sweetie pies a snake. We want to admonish using wisdom. By wisdom, we can conclude that we need to be gentle with our wives when we have a challenge to discuss.

When we take the gentle approach, we are less likely to elicit a negative response. In other words, she will less likely respond by calling you a low-life, snake-eating scumbag viper head.

The same applies to children. We need to correct them when they need correcting, but we want to make sure not to tear them down in the process. The Bible tells us, "Fathers, do not embitter your children, or they will become discouraged" (Colossians 3:21, NIV).

It is also written in scripture, "Fathers, do not exasperate your children; instead, bring them up in the training and instruction of the Lord" (Ephesians 6:4, NIV).

What does this have to do with your best wife now? I am glad you asked because even though blended families may not apply to you directly, you probably know someone who is in a blended family who might need to read this book.

Also if you are newly married to a woman who already has children then in order to keep your wife happy, you will need to know how to deal with the issues that arise in these newly married with children families.

I am trying to cover as many bases that I can think of so that the men of this world can have a happy family. So please recommend this book to all of your male friends whom you care about. Even if they aren't married yet, it won't hurt them to go ahead and start studying.

You can also use this book for a men's group at your church. Pastors can use it as part of their pre marriage counseling package. So please let your pastor know about this book.

As a stepparent, I must say I have had some hard times. I don't like the word step. To me, a parent is a parent. If you think about it, Jesus had a stepfather and stepsiblings, but I bet they didn't refer to each other as such. Our father in heaven does not refer to us as stepchildren.

Putting it all in one basket to make it easier to sort out, I want to say that if people are looking at you like you are a terrible person because you are a stepparent, let them look. Ignore these people because they do not live with you, and they are in no position to judge you. It is written in the Word of God,

> Brothers, do not slander one another. Anyone who speaks against his brother or judges him speaks against the law and judges it. When you judge the law, you are not keeping it, but sitting in judgment on it. There is only one Lawgiver and Judge, the one

who is able to save and to destroy. But you – who are
you to judge your neighbor?

James 4:11–12 (NIV)

As long as you are a righteous man, you can hold your
head up high. Your children may say you are mean, but if you
are not, people will know it, and if they don't believe you,
then so be it. Do not lose any sleep over it. Our Lord Jesus
sent us a comforter to give us peace, and that comforter is
the Holy Spirit. If we turn to the Holy Spirit, we will be
granted peace that surpasses all understanding.

Our God is not a God of confusion, but he is a God
of order. He loves us so much that he gave his only son
Jesus to die on the cross to provide forgiveness for our sins.
It is hard to imagine a love this strong isn't it? However,
when we accepted Jesus as our personal savior, we became
children of God.

He is my father in heaven, and when I need something,
I go to him and he gives it to me. If I need money, I ask
God in Jesus's name, and it is done. And my dad in heaven
has the largest wallet in the cosmos.

Points to Ponder
✓ Stepparents get a bad rap.
✓ I don't think that the world at large gives stepparents
a fair shake.
✓ People make a lot of assumptions that are
usually inaccurate.

- ✓ However, not all stepparents are good, but neither are all biological parents.
- ✓ If you marry a woman who has a kid or kids and you have been open and honest with your feelings about her children, then you can be a great parent.
- ✓ A stepparent has to build a relationship with the new child in his or her life, and both spouses should have already recognized this fact and should be good with it.
- ✓ At first it may be uncomfortable when your new wife corrects your child, just as it would be uncomfortable for her if you disciplined her child.
- ✓ Your biological children will look at you with an expression of "How could you let her do this to me Daddy?" This will bring out strong feelings.
- ✓ In fact, a couple may keep their feelings inside regarding the other parent's tactics for the first several months of their marriage. I say this is very unhealthy and dangerous to your marriage.
- ✓ If you don't let out your feelings as you go while the problems are small and manageable, then you might find yourself exploding at the woman you love six months or so down the road because you have been holding it in all that time, and just like a pressure cooker that couldn't hold the pressure, you blow up in your wife's face.

✓ This kind of explosion can cause lasting scars. It can cause your wife to walk on eggshells wondering when the next explosion will come.

✓ Your wife may do the same to you. She may explode on you from time to time.

✓ If you could both explain your true feelings as you go and use soft spoken words when you're doing it, I think you will have a lot less tension in the house.

✓ One thing my wife and I did in our family early on was to get rid of the word step. It has a negative feeling to it. We just don't use it. I have since adopted the only biological child of my wife we still have living at home.

✓ As long as you are a righteous man, you can hold your head up high, regardless of what others may say about you.

You Can't Get There From Here

Have you ever seen an alligator on the side of the road? Have you ever been to a Cajun family reunion? Have you ever been lost in the Duck Capital of Louisiana? Have you ever visited a graveyard while on a family vacation and had a blast doing it? If you answered yes to two or more of these questions, then you might just be a red-faced couple full of embarrassment because somebody had the map upside down.

Yep, it happened to my wife and me because somebody did have the map upside down and we turned left when we should have turned right. I'll explain this fun misadventure later, but first I would like to start from the top.

You see, my family, the Castille's from Louisiana, decided to have a family reunion several summers ago. At the time, we were a brand new family and hadn't had time to get mad at each other yet.

We were full of promise and happiness. This was our first road trip together and the first time for any of us to see or meet most of the Castille's (my relatives). The only family I knew up to that point was my Dad's brothers and sisters, along with their spouses and their children. So this was going to be new and exciting for all of us.

I had just married my wife; she already had three daughters and I already had one daughter, and we all piled into this big green rental van and set a course for gator country.

The van was a really nice ride; it had all the bells and whistles a man could want. I must admit it was a bit scary going from one kid to four kids in the blink of an eye. I viewed it in my mind as getting a little bag with tiny family members in it and placing it in the microwave and pushing the popcorn button. A few minutes later, all of the kernels had popped and presto, we had an instant family.

After a lovely drive with Dad at the wheel thinking he could sing and Mom reading a book wishing he could, with the teenager rocking out with her headphones on and the twenty-something just glad to be there while the two youngsters played in the way back. We finally arrived at my uncle's house.

When we pulled up, the kids were all starving but when they got out and saw the picnic table piled high with little crawfish staring at them, they suddenly lost their appetite. We took them to McDonald's; however, the McDonald's was somewhat Cajun-fide too. Some of the food they served was a little gamey according to the kids. I think they all lost weight on that particular vacation.

We got up the next day and got on the road toward the family reunion which was at a Veterans of Foreign War (VFW). We stopped a Cajun on the street and asked him if he knew where the Castille family reunion was and if he could give us directions. He said something like, "Can do easy, you just go down to where da road is, and go left. Den you go about four or tree blocks up dat road till you see a bunch of cars. But don't stop at da first bunch of cars where you see people eatin cause dat's not da reunion, dat's a funeral. What you want to do is go on to da next batch of cars where der is people what look like they are having fun eatin, and dat will be da place where da Castille family be at."

My kids had never heard a Cajun speak in that accent for real. They thought it was funny. They had to maintain their composure in the back of the van. We all got a good chuckle out of that one.

Consequently, this brings up my first point. Don't be afraid or too macho to ask for directions. Your wife probably doesn't have a problem stopping to ask. But as a man, I know we tend to have a bit of a problem admitting that we don't know where we are at half of the time. It is alright to be lost sometimes, it happens to the best of us. It happens to some of us more often than others, and I fall in to that category.

Just yesterday while traveling to the VA Hospital, my wife and I saw some birds flying south because it was bitterly cold outside. There were dozens of groups of birds all flying in v formations. But there was this one group of birds that were flying north, in the opposite direction of all of the other groups, and my wife said to me, "That group is probably being led by my husband." I must say I did resemble that remark.

Some people have a natural GPS (global positioning system) in their head and some people have an NGS (navigational guesser system) in their head. Guess which one I have?

So we made it to the reunion and we met a bunch of family members that we didn't know and ate a lot of food that we had never heard of. The kids appeared to be nervous and definitely out of their comfort zones. I guess it was a major case of culture shock.

As the reunion was winding down, the kids asked us if we could go see the Gulf of Mexico because they had never seen anything resembling an ocean. They had only seen a few West Texas stock tanks and of course many cement ponds. So we get some more directions and a map and head down the highway.

We are cruising along and we pass through the Frog Capital, the Rice Capital, the Sugarcane Capital, this and that capital, but we are not seeing the gulf. Finally, we get the map out and my oldest daughter finds the road we need to be on to get us to the water. She then hands the map to my queen who gets us to an intersection. She is looking at the map, and she says left takes us to the ocean. So we turn left.

We drive, and we drive, and we drive, and we do not see any ocean. We did pass by an interesting looking graveyard though. The graves were above ground because the area was real marshy and prone to flooding, and the caskets would just float up out of the ground and would not stay buried in this geographical location. So to prevent Uncle Boudreaux from floating away, they just buried him above ground where he can stay dry. The kids were fascinated because they had never seen graves such as these.

Finally, we saw a sign that said that we had made it to the Duck Capital of Louisiana. We pulled into a car wash and saw a man washing his truck. I rolled down my window and asked, "Excuse me sir, can you please tell me how to get to the Gulf of Mexico?" The man stopped what he was doing and gave me this look, like I would qualify for the world's biggest dummy contest. He then said, "You can't get there from here." He then uttered, "You done went as far as you possibly could in the wrong direction, and you're going to have to turn around and drive about tree or two hundred miles back down the road you just drove up here on."

So we turned around and headed back, by this time it was too late in the day to make it all the way to the gulf to see the water.

However, it was not too late to visit the graveyard that we had passed earlier. Upon arrival at the cemetery, the children disembarked the vehicle and proceeded to run around taking vast amounts of pictures at the different tomb sites. It was the most fun they had had all day.

When we got back on the road, my wife began to study the map with fervor and discovered that she had been looking at the map upside down earlier in the day when she had me turn left. This is how we got to the Duck Capital. What an adventure we had that day. It was a special time of bonding.

Having fun regardless of your surroundings is what life is all about. We still got to see the Gulf of Mexico the following day. As a husband, I could have gotten mad at my wife for having the map upside down. However, I had no right to because it was an honest mistake. I have heard of some husbands who yell at their wives on a regular basis for no reason. Even if we think we have a reason, I don't think yelling is a good option. Remember to try to be understanding, and to be happy, and to let go and let God.

Everybody is going to have bad times. We were not promised a trial-free life, especially as Christians, we are held to a high accountability. We will all be tested and the devil likes to hit us at the family level because if he can destroy the family, he can destroy the very fiber of the nation and the world.

This is why it is so important for us men to step it up a notch, to put our pride aside for our brides. Let us start focusing on building up our relationships with our wives.

The world needs us and if we answer the call, we can make the change.

The world is not going to get better all by itself. Yet we men have the power within us to build it back up from its very core. The core of this world is the family unit, and the core of the family unit is the husband and wife. Just think about it, if we put the values back in the families then the values will be put back into the world. It is still not too late, but almost.

So please, tell your wife you love her every day. Set a good example for the children to follow, so that when they get married, they will know how to have a strong, fulfilling relationship with their spouses. Our children watch our every move, and they model their lives based upon what they see.

Points to Ponder

- ✓ When traveling with your beauty queen and she is navigating, make sure she doesn't have the map upside down.
- ✓ Don't be afraid to stop and ask for directions. Even though in Cajun country you might not understand them, at least you will be entertained.
- ✓ You can be lost on the road and still have fun.
- ✓ My kids were starving until we arrived at my uncle's house and saw all the crawfish laid out on the picnic table. My uncle told them to dig in, and they dug right into the house with a request for a trip to McDonald's.

For Every Action, There Is a Reaction

I am pretty sure that we have all heard something similar to this. "For every action, there is a reaction." Now I know I probably left out a good portion of this theory, but I only need part of it for my best wife theory.

Here we go my friends this is not for the faint of heart.

ACTION	REACTION
Husband leaves the toilet lid up late at night	Wife gets wet and wakes up the neighborhood. She lectures till dawn.
Husband leaves underwear on floor	Wife gives him the eye. Then she lets him know she is not his maid, and will not be picking them up

Husband snores at night	Wife elbows him and tells him to roll over
Husband comes in past his curfew	Wife leaves his pillow on the couch
Husband plays video games all night	Wife feels unimportant
Husband never listens to wife	Wife becomes distant and quiet
Husband doesn't show affection	Wife expresses desire for contact
Husband addicted to porn	Wife feels unattractive and feels unwanted and withdraws.
Husband brings wife flowers	Wife feels important, loved and gives love in return
Husband shows affection	Wife shows affection in return.
Husband listens to wife	Wife feels important, relationship grows
Husband takes wife to dinner or does something special just to be with her.	Wife knows she is special and is content.

Do you kind of get the point? If you slap your wife in the face, she will probably slap you back. If you treat her like a queen, she will probably treat you like a king. Then you can both live in a royal family here on earth. We are already part of God's royal family—that is, if we are saved by the blood of our Lord Jesus.

This is not rocket science, I know, but you would be amazed at how many men out there treat their ladies like trash. I hope this book has helped some of you with some pointers on how to make some adjustments that will make your home a happier one.

Life is too short to live in constant strife. We have enough trouble to deal with out in the world, so our home life should be a life of peace and happiness.

When we come home and shut the door to the house, we are shutting the outside world out. If we want to unplug our phones, we can unplug our phones. We should make our homes places of retreat, so that we can get the rest that we really need in order to fight the issues that face us daily in this unforgiving, fast-paced, overinflated world.

The last thing we need is a poor relationship with our wife. After battling it out at work all day, the last thing we need to come home to is another battle.

I am telling you that if you take just a few simple steps, you can prevent these home front battles. If you work with your wife instead of against her, you will find that she makes a really strong coalition partner.

There is no one better at helping you fight your battles than your wife. Just put her on the phone and watch in amazement as she goes to work on the poor soul on the other end of the line.

When a man is on the phone, we just can't seem to get the same results as an irate woman can. Believe me, when I want to get something done, I hand the phone to my wife, and she gets the people hopping.

When God made Eve, he made for Adam a helpmate. So I think that it is time to stop arguing with the help and start giving them some praise and honoring them for all of the great things they do for us. If we are appreciative and don't take them for granted, then they will bend over backwards to help us and love us and be faithful to us.

It has been my observation that women are usually loyal in a marriage when their husband is treating them with respect, appreciation, and love. I have seen wives go out of their way to please husbands that were worthy of being pleased.

Also I would like to note than when a woman gets married, it is a serious event for her. She takes it seriously and has no plans for it to end prematurely. In fact, in most cases women tend to hang on even when they are married to complete jerks that don't deserve to be married in the first place. A woman is generally loyal to her husband.

Women normally won't consider a divorce unless there is infidelity involved or physical or severe mental abuse.

Sadly, I have heard of cases where women who have been physically beaten by their husbands would not leave them because they loved them. Although in a lot of cases, they stay in the relationship out of fear which is an absolutely horrible way to have to live.

It is my prayer that this book will turn thousands of marriages into happy and wonderful homes. Heck I pray that it turns a million marriages around for the better. I want to see nothing but happy marriages in this world. I am hoping that it starts with you.

Points to Ponder

- ✓ This chapter is pretty easy. You get out of your marriage what you put into it.
- ✓ You reap what you sow.
- ✓ I am praying that this book will turn thousands if not millions of families into happy and wonderful homes.
- ✓ I want to see nothing but happy marriages in this world.
- ✓ I am hoping that it starts with you.

Socks

In Spanish, s-o-c-k-s means that's what it is. This chapter is my explanation of how my wife feels about socks. By the way, my wife just ordered us a "How to Speak Spanish" course via the internet, and we are in the process of learning Spanish as a second language.

Furthermore, my kids went on a mission trip to Mexico, and they learned a few Spanish words while they were there. The point being that we are planning to be prepared for future mission trips to Mexico and other Spanish-speaking regions of the world.

My wife said to me as she slaved over a mountain of socks: "Socks should be made to disintegrate after four wears. That way, we would not wind up with a huge pile of socks to try to match. We could just keep buying new ones." I should mention that we have daughters who either wear their mother's socks or they wash them, and then mismatch them, and place them in the wrong drawers. For instance,

I end up with my wife's socks in my drawers, and my wife ends up with my socks in her drawers.

This really steams my wife. She gets really upset when anyone other than her matches the socks. We tend to not pay close enough attention to detail. If two socks look remotely similar, they get put together. Apparently, it just does not bother my kids and me to wander around in mismatched socks. That's what it is, that's the way it is, and that's the way we see it.

Unfortunately though for us is that Mom carries with her a strong, invisible force that she can unleash upon the rest of us poor unsuspecting souls. When we least expect it, we find ourselves standing tall on the carpet getting the sock lecture. We then find ourselves being strongly warned not to get near the socks, not to wash the socks, and definitely not to put the socks in drawers.

I know that this is a short chapter, but I felt led to tell the world to stay away from the socks if you know what is good for you. I know we men don't care if our socks match or not, but the wife does. I know that what we see as just a trivial little thing is looked at from a much more serious, much more dangerous point of view from the other sex.

It is not a good idea to ignore your queen when she is unloading what you may think is unimportant ramblings about insignificant topics. Your wife needs you to listen and look concerned while you are listening. She does not require you to comment. In fact, I do not advise it. If she wants your opinion, she will give it to you.

All you have to do is stay silent and look concerned and no one will get hurt. Women just need to get their feelings out. They may not make any sense to you, but somehow they make sense to themselves and that is what is important.

If you try to butt in and make a comment, it totally disrupts her train of thought, and yes it is a train, and the cars do link together in an order that only she can understand. But it has to come out of her or it will be twice as bad the next time.

I used to get upset when my wife would go off in a tangent about a topic that did not make any sense to me. It stressed me out because I would try to understand what she was saying, and I would try to make what I thought were helpful comments. Guess what my friends? There is no such thing as a helpful comment when your queen is venting. She may be talking about three different things and switching back and forth between topics and you may be totally confused but believe me she knows exactly where she leaves off of each topic and can pick it up without missing a beat.

She can also be talking to you, talking to her mother on the phone, surfing the net, hollering for the kids to do the dishes, reading a book, painting her nails, soaking her feet, folding socks, and chewing gum all at the same time.

Men tend to try to stay on one task at a time. If we are on the phone, and our wife asks us a question, our brains shut down and we cease to function. If you added a piece of bubble gum to the equation, then you might as well call for an ambulance because we would probably go into shock. We like to handle one thing at a time. That is just the way it is. Am I right?

It is just so amazing how different we can be. However, it is this difference that makes us work together. God made the man and the woman to coexist in harmony. When sin entered the world in the Garden of Eden, then we started seeing strife between mankind in general. For instance, Adam and Eve's son Cain killed Abel. Can you imagine being recorded as the first man to commit murder?

Well, I am sure Adam and Eve had some pretty good arguments after they ate the fruit of the tree of the knowledge of good and evil. It was a sad day for us all. It was not until after the sin that they even realized that they were naked. If they had not sinned, then there would be no such a thing as a sock, and I would not even be writing this chapter.

God spoke to Moses in the burning bush and told him to go get the Pharaoh to let his people go. Then after that happened, he gave the law to Moses to give to man. Even then, mankind could not follow these rules which included the Ten Commandments. So there continued to be strife in the world.

Then one day, a child was born to a virgin mother Mary, and he was the Son of God. He was sent here to teach us that there would be a new way to reach the father and that was through him. As an adult, he healed the sick, raised the dead, gave sight to the blind, and ultimately gave his life for the atonement of our sins. Now we who believe in him shall not perish but have life everlasting. When we invite Jesus into our hearts, we are born again and become dead to sin. We are given a way to Father God's throne through him.

Now when a man and a woman get married, there is a way to live in harmony with one another. For when Jesus ascended into heaven after he had been crucified and rose from the dead, he told his disciples that he would send a comforter that would offer us a peace that would surpass all understanding.

This would be the Holy Spirit. If we ask Jesus into our hearts and become saved, and begin to live our lives according to God's will, then and only then can we have a peaceful marriage.

However, if you are of this world and you are not saved, then no matter how hard you try to have a good marriage, you will always feel emptiness inside, and you will leave yourself open to the deception of the enemy, the devil, who roams to and fro, seeking whom he can destroy. He will try every trick in the book to make your life miserable. He will tempt you to cheat on your wife, and he will tempt you to lust for other women, which Jesus said is the same as sleeping with them.

Even as a Christian, we are subject to trials and temptations; however, it is written that we will not be tempted beyond our ability to escape. The Lord will always leave an escape route when the enemy is in your midst, trying to get you to stumble and fall. See 1 Corinthians 10:13. Don't fall for his tricks. Listen with your spiritual ears to what God is trying to convey to you as you go through your days and nights. He will tell you when something is not right. The Holy Spirit will guide you through life and marriage and give you fulfillment emotionally, spiritually, and physically.

The best sex is between a husband and a wife in love, and who are children of God. God gave us sex as a gift that is only to be shared in the marriage union of a husband and a wife. It may sound like a fun idea to sleep around and try out every woman you can get your hands on, but this will only bring discontentment into your life.

I know that there will be times when your wife is going on and on about socks, or your snoring, or the way you load the dishwasher that you might want to trade her in for a new model.

This is not the answer though because guess what? The new model would find something to go on about. It is just the nature of marriage. When we realize this and learn to accept it, then we will finally be able to gain control of our relationships.

All you have to do is listen every now and then. All you have to do is to let your wife know that she is important and special to you. You need to take care of her physical and emotional needs to make your marriage a success. You need to realize that just because something is not important to you or does not bother you that it may be important to your wife. Don't put her down because you don't think her problems, and feelings are important. Remember as men we don't get excited about the same things women do.

Underwear on the floor, whiskers in the sink, a ring around the bathtub, dirty drinking glasses all over the house, a hole in the roof, and a drawer full of mismatched socks may not bother us men, but they sure as heck do bother women.

So if we can just keep this in mind when the wife starts going on about something, maybe we could finally learn to pinpoint the root cause and then listen to what she says and finally take actions to make a few changes to rectify the situation.

We knew the job was going to be tough when we took it. So let's be men and get to work at sticking with one woman—the woman that made our knees weak the first time we laid eyes on her; the woman that made our tongue get all twisted and tangled the first time we asked her out; and the woman that made our hearts flutter the first time we held hands or gave her a smack right on the kisser.

Remember that wedding night when you went some place special and joined together as one. God put you together for a reason. You truly are a match made in heaven.

Please don't devalue the union that God has made. He has a plan for you and your wife. When God looks down from heaven, he doesn't see two people; he sees one. His word says that when a man and a woman get married, they become one flesh and your wife's body is no longer hers but yours. Your body is no longer yours but hers. So if you think about it, anything you do wrong to her, you are doing it to yourself.

So keep your socks on pilgrim. If you take them off and they get washed, make sure they get back together again and put in the correct chest of drawers. Put God first in your marriage and listen to his Holy Spirit. He will lead you along the good path. He will lead you along the path that leads to life everlasting. He will ensure that you have *your best wife now!*

Points to Ponder

✓ Unless you are highly trained, it might be a good idea to stay away from the socks.

✓ Even though we may think that because we observe a basketful of all white, similar looking socks, that matching them should be a piece of cake, think again.

✓ This is wrong, my wife systematically examines each fiber of each sock and she can tell within just a few microfibers what sock matches what.

- ✓ If I attempt to do the same thing, I fail to get it right, time after time I fail.
- ✓ It is just better to leave the socks alone if your wife is hypersensitive to the darn things.
- ✓ There may be times when your wife is getting on to you about the socks, or the way you loaded the dishwasher, or whatever, and you may be thinking of trading her in for a new model.
- ✓ Trading her in is not the way to go because your new wife will have a whole list of things that bother her too.
- ✓ We need to realize that men and women are wired differently and that what doesn't bother you may bug the heck out of your wife. Things in the home bother the wife, she wants her home to be nice, neat, and clean.
- ✓ Getting along is not as hard as some people make it. I am sure that you will do just fine.
- ✓ Follow God and listen to the Holy Spirit. He will lead you and guide you into a peace that surpasses all understanding. He will help you to have your best wife now!

About the Author

Jason Castille graduated from Liberty University receiving a B.S. in Religion, double minor in Christian Counseling and Church Ministry and graduated with honors; cum laude. He is currently in a Master's program. He pastored New River Ministries in Abilene, Texas until 2011. He is currently spreading the gospel through his books and speaking engagements and conferences. He lives in Abilene with his wife Rebecca; together they have raised four amazing daughters. Jason is available for special engagements and speaking engagements, for more information he can be contacted at email: pastorjason@risingpointministries.org

Please Contact Us

Rebecca and I would love to hear from you. If you need prayer let us know. If you have a comment about the book, please let us know. If you are not sure about your salvation and you need someone to pray with you about asking Jesus into your life and heart, let us know. We will stand in prayer with you.